Amazing Wo...

HERSTORY

Maria Skłodowska-Curie, 1898
Soure: Wikimedia
Artist: Unknown
License: Public Domain

OFFICIAL BIOGRAPHY

The Official Girl Guide to Marie Curie

Dedicated to Frank and Sayaka's
amazing daughters Skye and Meadow.
Remember ladies...

Life is a gift you give another.
Learning is a gift you give yourself.
Loving is a gift you give the world.

The Official Girl Guide to Marie Curie

The Official Girl Guide to Marie Curie

Lovingly Authored By:
Dr. Manako Kamisawa

ISBN: 9781795656108

The Official Girl Guide to Marie Curie

Contents

Official Fact Book of MarieCurie 1

    Birth Facts 2

    In the year of Her Birth 3

    End of Life Facts 4

    In the Year of Her Death 5

    Major Awards 6

    Historical Quotations 7

    Interesting Fact Hall of Fame 8

Official Biography of MarieCurie 18

1 Early life & Place and date of birth 19

2 Family 25

3 Childhood 31

4 Early Life and Education 40

5 Marie Curie's Scientific Discoveries 45

    Why Uranium? 46

    Discovery of Polonium, Radium and a New Word 49

    Work in Paris 51

    Recognition 56

    End of an era 59

4 Fame 63

    She created a place for women in science 70

    Most challenging 72

    Top Student Again 74

    Homesick 75

    Tragedy and Progress 76

    Meeting Pierre Curie 77

    A Ph.D. and a Nobel Prize in Physics! 83

Nobel Prize for Chemistry ....,,,,,84

5 Later life 86

6 Legacy 90

International Society Of Young Scientists and Engineers

Official
Fact Book
of
MarieCurie

The Official Girl Guide to Marie Curie

Birth Facts

Source: OpenStreetMap.org

Name at Birth: Maria Salomea Skłodowska
Birth Date: November 7th, 1867
Birth Country: Poland
Birth City: Warsaw
Mother: Bronisława
Father: Władysław

In the year of Her Birth

What happened the same year as the birth of MarieCurie?

Fact #1
US buys Alaska from Russia for $7,200,000 (2 cents an acre - Seward's Folly)

Fact #2
African American men granted the right to vote in Washington, D.C. despite President Andrew Johnson's veto.

Fact #3
Jesse James gang robs bank in Richmond, Missouri (2 die, $4,000 taken).

Fact #4
Nov 25 Swedish chemist, Alfred Nobel, patents dynamite.

Fact #5
Laura Ingalls Wilder is born.

End of Life Facts

Source: OpenStreetMap.org

Name at Death: MarieCurie
Death Date: July, 4th 1934
Death Country: Poland
Death City: Paris

In the Year of Her Death

What happened the same year as the death of MarieCurie?

Fact #1
The Flash Gordon comic strip is first published, in the United States.

Fact #2
London doctor Robert Kenneth Wilson takes a photograph of the Loch Ness Monster. However, in 1994 it is proved to be an elaborate hoax.

Fact #3
Adolf Hitler and Benito Mussolini meet for the first time, at the Venice Biennale.

Fact #4
Persia becomes Iran.

Fact #5
"It Happened One Night" directed by Frank Capra and starring Clark Gable and Claudette Colbert opens at NY's Radio City Music Hall.

Major Awards

Award #1
Nobel Prize in Physics, 1903

Award #2
Elliott Cresson Medal, 1909

Award #3
Albert Medal, 1910

Award #4
Nobel Prize in Chemistry, 1911

Historical Quotations

Quotation #1
Nothing in life is to be feared, it is only to be understood. Now is the time to understand more, so that we may fear less.

Quotation #2
Be less curious about people and more curious about ideas.

Quotation #3
Have no fear of perfection; you'll never reach it.

Quotation #4
You cannot hope to build a better world without improving the individuals. To that end, each of us must work for our own improvement.

Interesting Fact
Hall of Fame

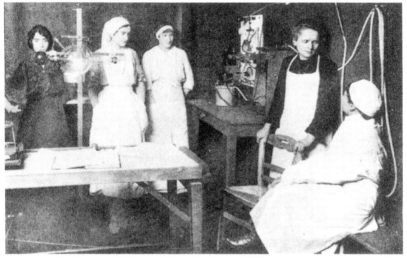

Marie Curie with nurses and doctor, 1915

Source: Wikimedia
Photographer: Unknown
License: Public Domain

SHE DID PART-TIME WORK WHILE COMPLETING HER EDUCATION

Marie was not allowed to enrol in a higher education institution in Russia-occupied Warsaw because she was a female. So Marie and her sister, Bronya, continued their education in the Flying University, a clandestine pro Polish institution in defiance of Russian authority. They made a pact that Marie would give financial assistance to Bronya during her medical studies in Paris and Bronya would return the favour when she completed her course. In connection to this, Marie worked as a tutor and governess for roughly five years, all the while sparing time to educate herself in physics, chemistry and mathematics.

DUE TO SHORTAGE OF MONEY, SHE OCCASIONALLY FAINTED FROM HUNGER

In 1891, Marie moved to Paris and enrolled in Sorbonne (the University of Paris) to pursue her studies of physics, chemistry and mathematics. She studied during the day and tutored in the evening. With little money, she survived on buttered bread and tea, and occasionally fainted from hunger. In 1893, Marie was awarded a degree in Physics and the following year she earned another degree in mathematics.

MARIA MET PIERRE CURIE BECAUSE SHE WAS LOOKING FOR LARGER LABORATORY SPACE

In mid 1890s, Marie began her scientific career and was searching for larger laboratory space. Professor Jozef Wierusz-Kowalski introduced Marie to Pierre Curie as he thought that Pierre had such a space. Though he did not have a large laboratory, Pierre was able to find some space for Marie to begin her work. Their mutual interest in science drew Maria and Pierre closer and a romance ensued. In July 1895, Marie married Pierre Curie in a civil union as they didn't want a religious service. Marie's dark blue outfit, worn instead of a bridal grown, would serve her for many years as a lab outfit.

MARIE CURIE PROVED THAT ATOMS WERE DIVISIBLE

After French physicist, Henri Becquerel, first discovered a strange source of energy coming from uranium that resembled X-rays in their penetrating power, Marie Curie decided that this would make a good field for research. During her research, Marie made several scientific discoveries. She came to know that the activity of uranium depended only on the quantity of uranium present and that radiation did indeed come from the atom itself rather than an interaction between molecules. This disproved the ancient assumption that atoms were indivisible; and led to the creation of atomic physics.

THE CURIES COINED THE WORD RADIOACTIVITY

In 1898, Marie Curie discovered that thorium was also radioactive but she was beaten in the race to tell of her discovery by Gerhard Schmidt, who published it two months earlier. In the same year Pierre Curie decided that he would join Marie in her work. In July 1898, they published a paper together announcing the existence of an element which they named "polonium", in honour of her native country Poland. Then in December, the Curies announced the existence of a second element, which they named "radium" from the Latin word for ray.In the course of their research, they also coined the word radioactivity.

INITIALLY, THE NOBEL PRIZE COMMITTEE DIDN'T WANT THE AWARD TO BE GIVEN TO MARIE AS SHE WAS A WOMAN

In December 1903, Marie Curie became the first woman to be awarded the Nobel Prize, when along with her husband and Henri Becquerel, she was awarded the Nobel Prize in Physics "in recognition of the extraordinary services they have rendered by their joint research on the radiation phenomena discovered by Professor Henri Becquerel." Initially, the Committee did not want to recognize the contribution of Marie Curie but her husband was informed of this by a committee member, who was also an advocate of women scientists. Upon a complaint by Pierre, his wife's name was added to the nomination.

MARIE CURIE IS THE ONLY PERSON TO WIN NOBEL PRIZES IN MULTIPLE SCIENCES

On 19 April 1906, Pierre Curie was killed in Paris after he accidentally stepped in front of a horse-drawn wagon. Although she was devastated, Marie took over his teaching post at the Sorbonne, becoming the institution's first female professor. In 1910, Marie succeeded in isolating radium and also defined an international standard for radioactive emissions which was eventually named after her and Pierre: the curie. A year later, Marie was awarded a second Nobel Prize, this time for Chemistry "in recognition of her services to the advancement of chemistry by the discovery of the elements radium and polonium, by the isolation of radium and the study of the nature and compounds of this remarkable element." She became the first person to win or share two

Nobel Prizes and remains the only one who has won it in multiple sciences. She is also the only woman and one of only two people to win a Nobel Prize in two different fields.

Nobel Prize, 911
Source: Wikimedia
License: Public Domain

MARIE CURIE DIED DUE TO HER WORK

In 1934, Curie went to the Sancellemoz Sanatorium in Passy, France, to try to rest and regain her strength. She died there on July 4th, 1934, of aplastic anemia, which can be caused by prolonged exposure to radiation. The damaging effects of ionising radiation were not known at the time of her work, which had been carried out without the safety measures later developed. She had carried test tubes containing radioactive isotopes in her pocket and stored them in her desk drawer. Because of their levels of radioactivity, her papers from the 1890s are considered too dangerous to handle. They are kept in lead-lined boxes, and those who wish to consult them must wear protective clothing.

International Society Of
Young Scientists and Engineers

Official
Biography
of
MarieCurie

1
Early life & Place and date of birth

Marie Sklodowska Curie, popularly known as Marie

Curie, was born on November 7, 1867 in Warsaw,

Poland. Although Curie has a Polish upbringing, she

eventually acquired French citizenship and was a

famous chemist and physicist whose pioneering

works in radioactivity earned her two Nobel

Prizes both in chemistry and physics. She was also

considered as the first female professor who

taught at the University of Paris.

Curie spent the first 24 years of her life in

Poland. Then, in 1891, she moved to Bronisawa to continue her higher degrees in Paris and conducted her scientific works. She established her Curie Institutes in Paris and Warsaw.

Members of her family were all Nobel Peace Prize Awardees as well. She shared her Nobel Peace Prize in Physics with her husband Pierre Curie. In addition, her own daughter Irène Joliot-Curie and her husband Frédéric Joliot-Curie, also shared the prestigious Nobel prize awards.

Curie was regarded as the person behind the theory of radioactivity. Her techniques isolated the radioactive isotopes and she discovered the existence of two new elements, Radium and

Polonium. Her group was also responsible for conducting the first treatment of cancer by using radioactive isotopes in the history of mankind.

Unusually for women at that time, Marya took an interest in Chemistry and Biology. Since opportunities in Poland for further study were limited, Marya went to Paris, where after working as a governess she was able to study at the Sorbonne, Paris. Struggling to learn in French, Marya threw herself into her studies, leading an ascetic life dedicated to education and improving her scientific knowledge. She went on to get a degree in Physics and finished top of her class. She later got a degree in Maths, finishing second in her school year. Curie had a remarkable willingness for hard work.

Although she had acquired French citizenship, her Polish identity was never lost. In fact, she named the new element she discovered as "Polonium" after her home country, Poland. In 1932, she also established Radium Institute now known as Maria Sklodowska-Curie Institute of Oncology in Warsaw, her hometown.

Dr. Curie is primarily known for her discovery of Radium and Polonium. She also discovered that x-rays were able to kill tumors and was the first person to win two Nobel prizes. Marie Curie decided not to obtain patents for the processing of radium and the medical applications

applicable to it.

"Life is not easy for any of us.But what of

that? We must have perseverance and above all

confidence in ourselves. We must believe that we

are gifted for something, and that this thing, at

whatever cost, must be attained."

It was in Paris that she met Pierre Curie,

who was then chief of the laboratory at the

School of Physics and Chemistry. He was a

renowned Chemist, who had conducted many

experiments on crystals and electronics. Pierre

was smitten with the young Marya and asked her

to marry him. Marya initially refused but, after

persistence from Pierre, she relented.Until

Pierre's untimely death in 1906, the two were

inseparable. In addition to co-operation on work,

they spent much leisure time bicycling and

travelling around Europe together.

2
Family

Skłodowski family: Władysław and his
Daughters : Maria, Bronisława, Helena
Source: Wikimedia
Photographer: Unknown
License: Public Domain

The seventh of November, 1867, was a special day for Sklodowska as the couple was blessed with their last of five children, a daughter, whom they named Marya. Marya was lovingly called Manya by her parents, brother and sisters all through her life but to the rest of the world she was Marie Curie. Marya's parents had no clue that their youngest daughter would make history with her achievements and have an amazing future ahead. Marya's family was an educated family of teachers who stayed in 19th century Poland. Her paternal grandfather, Jozef Skldowski, had been a respected teacher in Lublin and her father, Vladislav Sklodowska, was a Polish teacher who taught Mathematics and Physics and managed several schools and reformatory for boys. He was a very well-read and knowledgeable individual who was regarded as a 'walking encyclopedia' by his children. Marya's mother, Bronislawa, was a teacher and the headmistress of a girl's school in Warsaw; capital and largest city of Poland. She wielded tremendous influence on the minds and lives of all her children. Marya's father was an atheist whereas her mother, a devout Catholic.

She was a supermom of her time and it is said that she even made shoes for all her children with her own hands. She was a woman of great beauty and intelligence, who could handle all her

tasks with finesse. The Sklodowska family was

very scholarly and cultured and these values were

passed on to their children who imbibed them well.

In their early years, Marie and her siblings

had a comfortable and happy childhood, with

exciting holidays in the countryside with their

relatives, and lots of love and attention from

their parents. But life is transient, so are the

moments of happiness and each one of us has to

experience the rollercoaster ride of ups and

downs in life.

After her father lost his job, the family

struggled and was forced to take borders

(renters) into their small apartment. Religious as a child, Curie rejected her faith after her sister died of typhus (a severe fever) in 1876. Two years later she lost her mother to tuberculosis, a terrible disease that attacks the lungs and bones.

Both of Marie Curie's parents were teachers, and she was the youngest of five children, following siblings Zosia, Józef, Bronya and Hela. As a child, Curie took after her father, Wladyslaw, a math and physics instructor. She had a bright and curious mind and excelled at school. However, tragedy struck early: When she was only 10, Curie lost her mother, Bronislawa, to tuberculosis.

In early 1886, Marie accepted a job as governess (private educator) with a family living in Szczuki, Poland, but the intellectual loneliness she experienced there only solidified her determination to somehow achieve her dream of becoming a university student. One of her sisters, Bronya, was already in Paris, France, successfully passing the examinations in medicine.In September 1891, Marie moved in with her sister in Paris.

3
Childhood

Maria Sklodowska, 1883
Source: Wikimedia
Photographer: Unknown
License: Public Domain

From childhood, she was remarkable for her

prodigious memory, and at the age of 16 she won a

gold medal on completion of her secondary education at the Russian lycée. Because her father, a teacher of mathematics and physics, lost his savings through bad investment, she had to take on work as a teacher and, at the same time, took part clandestinely in the nationalist "free university," reading in Polish to women workers. At the age of 18 she took a post as governess, where she suffered an unhappy love affair. From her earnings, she was able to finance her sister, Bronisława's medical studies in Paris, with the understanding that Bronisława would in turn later help her to acquire an education.

In the late 19th century when Marie was

born, Poland was a complex and tough place to reside in. In the 1790s, Poland was invaded by its greedy neighbours - Russia, Austria and Prussia. Poland was a weak nation then and was annexed by these powerful countries which divided it among themselves for power and pelf. The northern part of Poland, where Marie and her family resided, was occupied by Russia and it also included the capital city of Warsaw. The Polish people had attempted to overthrow their tormentors on several occasions but were unsuccessful and were either executed or banished to Siberia if they ever dared to rebel their authority. The entire Polish life was thrown out of gear due to the incursion of policemen, professors and minor

dignitaries from Russia.These Russians were

watchful of even the smallest traces of rebellion

like the speaking of Polish language or an

indiscreet word about them. Polish intellectuals

and teachers were not allowed to openly express

their ideas and were told to teach only in Russian

language and not in Polish. Life was so difficult for

the Poles that they could not even practise their

Catholic religion without the fear of being

attacked by the Russians. The Polish children were

forced to learn Russian history and Russian folk

tales in school.Due to this scenario, there was a

lot of resentment and unrest in the country which

was the homeland to Marie Curie. Marie would

often dream of a free nation where all could live

happily and peacefully and thus progress well.

Maria and her older sister, Bronia, both

wished to attend college but the University of

Warsaw did not accept women. They were both

interested in scientific research; but to get the

education they desired, they would have to leave

the country. At the age of 17, Maria became a

governess to help pay for Bronia to attend

medical school in Paris. Maria continued to study

on her own, looking forward to joining her sister

and getting her own degree.

When Maria registered at the Sorbonne, in Paris,

she signed her name as "Marie" to seem more French. She realized her high school education and self-study had not prepared her for the Sorbonne. She had planned to live with Bronia, but took a drafty garret apartment closer to the school so she would have more time to study. To afford the rent, she often subsisted only on bread and tea. Her health suffered, but the hard work paid off. When it was time for the final examinations, she was first in her class. She earned her master's degree in physics in July 1893. Women's education advocates gave her a scholarship to stay and take a second degree in mathematics, awarded in 1894.

In 1891, Skłodowska went to Paris and, now using the name Marie, began to follow the lectures of Paul Appel, Gabriel Lippmann, and Edmond Bouty at the Sorbonne. There she met physicists who were already well known—Jean Perrin, Charles Maurain, and Aimé Cotton. Skłodowska worked far into the night in her student-quarters garret and virtually lived on bread and butter and tea.She came first in the licence of physical sciences in 1893.She began to work in Lippmann's research laboratory and in 1894 was placed second in the licence of mathematical sciences.It was in the spring of that year that she met Pierre Curie.

A top student in her secondary school, Curie could not attend the men's-only University of Warsaw. She instead continued her education in Warsaw's "floating university," a set of underground, informal classes held in secret. Both Curie and her sister Bronya dreamed of travelling abroad to earn an official degree, but they lacked the financial resources to pay for more schooling. Undeterred, Curie worked out a deal with her sister. She would work to support Bronya while she was in school and Bronya would return the favor after she completed her studies. For roughly five years, Curie worked as a tutor and a governess.She used her spare time to study, reading about physics, chemistry and math.

In 1891, Curie finally made her way to Paris and enrolled at the Sorbonne. She threw herself into her studies, but this dedication had a personal cost. With little money, Curie survived on buttered bread and tea, and her health sometimes suffered because of her poor diet. Curie completed her master's degree in physics in 1893 and earned another degree in mathematics the following year.

4
Early Life and Education

Marie, Pierre and Irène Curie, 1902
Source: Wikimedia
Photographer: Unknown
License: Public Domain

Maria Salomea Sklodowska was born in

Warsaw, Poland on November 7, 1867. At that

time, Warsaw lay within the borders of the

Russian Empire. Maria's family wanted Poland to be an independent country.

Marie's mother and father – Bronislawa and Wladyslaw – were both teachers and encouraged her interest in science.

When Marie was aged 10, her mother died. Marie started attending a boarding school, then moved to a gymnasium – a selective school for academically strong children. Aged 15, Marie graduated from high school, winning the gold medal for top student. She was passionate about science and wanted to continue learning about it.

Marie married French physicist Pierre Curie on July 26, 1895. They were introduced by a colleague of Marie's after she graduated from the

University of Sorbonne; Marie had received a

commission to perform a study on different types

of steel and their magnetic properties and needed

a lab to work in. A romance developed between the

brilliant pair, and they became a scientific dynamic

duo who were completely devoted to one another.

At first, Marie and Pierre worked on separate

projects. But after Marie discovered

radioactivity, Pierre put aside his own work to help

her with her research.

In 1897 Marie and Pierre Curie welcomed a

daughter, Irène. The couple had a second

daughter, Ève, in 1904. Irène Joliot-Curie

followed in her mother's footsteps, winning the Nobel Prize in Chemistry in 1935. Joliot-Curie shared the honor with her husband, Frédéric Joliot, for their work on the synthesis of new radioactive elements.

Marie suffered a tremendous loss in 1906, when Pierre died in Paris after accidentally stepping in front of a horse-drawn wagon. Despite her tremendous grief, she took over his teaching post at the Sorbonne, becoming the institution's first female professor.

In 1911, Marie Curie's relationship with her husband's former student, Paul Langevin, became public. Curie was derided in the press for breaking up Langevin's marriage, the negativity in part

stemming from rising xenophobia in France.

5
Marie Curie's Scientific Discoveries

The Ph.D. degree is a research based degree,

and Marie Curie now began investigating the

chemical element uranium.

Marie and Pierre Curie (centre), 1904

Source: Wellcome Collection gallery (2018-03-31
Photographer: Unknown
License: CC BY 4.0

Why Uranium?

In 1895, Wilhelm Roentgen had discovered mysterious X-rays, which could capture photographs of human bones beneath skin and muscle.

The following year, Henri Becquerel had discovered that rays emitted by uranium could pass through metal, but Becquerel's rays were not X-rays.

Marie decided to investigate the rays from uranium – this was a new and very exciting field to work in. Discoveries came to her thick and fast. She discovered that:

Uranium rays electrically charge the air they pass through. Such air can conduct electricity. Marie detected this using an electrometer Pierre and his brother had invented.

The number of rays coming from uranium depends only on the amount of uranium present – not the chemical form of the uranium. From this, she theorized correctly that the rays came from within the uranium atoms and not from a chemical reaction.

The uranium minerals, pitchblende and torbernite, have more of an effect on the conductivity of air than pure uranium does.She theorized correctly that these minerals must contain another chemical element, more active than uranium.

The chemical element, thorium, emits rays in the same way as uranium. (Gerhard Carl Schmidt in Germany actually discovered this a few weeks before Marie Curie in 1898: she discovered it independently.)

By the summer of 1898, Marie's husband Pierre had become as excited about her discoveries as Marie herself. He asked Marie if he could cooperate with her scientifically, and she welcomed him. By this time, they had a one-year old daughter, Irene. Amazingly, 37 years later, Irene Curie herself would win the Nobel Prize in Chemistry.

Discovery of Polonium, Radium and a New Word

Marie and Pierre decided to hunt for the new element they suspected might be present in pitchblende. By the end of 1898, after laboriously processing tons of pitchblende, they announced the discovery of two new chemical elements which would soon take their place in Dmitri Mendeleev's periodic table.

The first element they discovered was polonium, named by Marie to honor her homeland. They found that polonium was 300 times more radioactive than uranium. They wrote:

"We thus believe that the substance that we have

extracted from pitchblende contains a metal

never known before, akin to bismuth in its analytic

properties. If the existence of this new metal is

confirmed, we suggest that it should be called

polonium after the name of the country of origin

of one of us."

The second element the couple discovered was

radium, which they named after the Latin word

for ray. The Curies found that radium is several

million times more radioactive than uranium! They

also found that radium's compounds are luminous

and that radium is a source of heat, which it

produces continuously without any chemical reaction taking place.Radium is always hotter than its surroundings.

Together they came up with a new word for the phenomenon they were observing: radioactivity. Radioactivity is produced by radioactive elements such as uranium, thorium, polonium and radium.

Work in Paris

When classes began at the Sorbonne in Paris in early November 1891, Marie enrolled as a student of physics. By 1894 she was desperately

looking for a laboratory where she could work on

her research project, the measurement of the

magnetic properties of various steel alloys (metal

mixtures). Acting upon a suggestion, she visited

Pierre Curie at the School of Physics and

Chemistry at the University of Paris. In 1895,

Pierre and Marie were married, thus beginning a

most extraordinary partnership in scientific work.

By mid-1897, Curie's scientific achievements were

two university degrees, a fellowship (a

scholarship), and a monograph (published paper)

on the magnetization of tempered steel. The

couple's first daughter, Irène, had just been

born, and it was then that the Curies turned their

attention to the mysterious radiation from uranium recently discovered by Antoine Henri Becquerel (1852-1908). It was Marie's hunch that the radiation was an atomic property, and therefore had to be present in some other elements as well. Her search soon established the fact of a similar radiation from thorium, and she invented the historic word "radioactivity" (the spontaneous release of radium).

While searching for other sources of radioactivity, the Curies had turned their attention to pitchblende, a mineral well known for its uranium content. To their immense surprise, the radioactivity of pitchblende far exceeded the combined radioactivity of the uranium and thorium contained in it.

From their laboratory, two papers reached the Academy of Sciences within six months. The first, read at the meeting of July 18, 1898, announced the discovery of a new radioactive element, which the Curies named polonium after Marie's native country. The other paper, announcing the discovery of radium, was read at the December 26 meeting.

From 1898 to 1902, the Curies converted several tons of pitchblende, but it was not only the extremely precious centigrams of radium that rewarded their superhuman efforts. The Curies also published, jointly or separately, during those

years a total of thirty-two scientific papers.

Among them, one announced that diseased, tumor-

forming cells were destroyed faster than healthy

cells when exposed to radium.

Recognition

First Solvay Conference on Physics, Brussels, 1911
Source: Wikimedia
Photographer: Unknown
License: Public Domain

In November 1903, the Royal Society of

London gave the Curies one of its highest awards,

the Davy Medal. A month later followed the

announcement from the Nobel Foundation in

Stockholm, Sweden, that three French scientists,

A. H. Becquerel and the Curies, were the joint

recipients of the Nobel Prize in Physics for 1903.

Finally, even the academics in Paris began to stir,

and a few months later, Marie was appointed

director of research at the University of Paris.

In December 1904, their second daughter,

Ève, was born. The next year brought the election

of Pierre to the Academy of Sciences and their

travel to Stockholm, where, on June 6, he

delivered the Nobel Prize lecture, which was in

fact their joint address. Pierre ended his speech

with the double-edged impact on mankind of every

major scientific advance. Pierre said that he

believed "mankind will derive more good than harm

from the new discoveries."

End of an era

The joyful time for this husband-and-wife team would not last long. On the rainy mid-afternoon of April 19, 1906, Pierre was run down by a heavy carriage and killed instantly.

Two weeks later, the widow was asked to take over her late husband's post. Honors began to pour in from scientific societies all over the world on a woman left alone with two small children and with whom the gigantic task of leadership in radioactivity research was now left.

In 1908, she edited the collected works of her late husband, and in 1910 she published her massive Traité de radioactivité. Shortly after this work, Curie received her second Nobel Prize, this time in chemistry. Still, Curie was unable to win over the Academy of Sciences, who once again denied her membership.

Curie devoted much of her time during World War I (1914–18) to equipping automobiles in her own laboratory, the Radium Institute, with x-ray (Roentgen) apparatus to assist the sick. It was these cars that became known in the war zone as "little Curies."

By the end of the war, Curie was past her fiftieth year, with much of her physical energy already spent—along with her savings, which she had patriotically invested in war bonds.But her

dedication was inexhaustible.

The year 1919 witnessed her installation at

the Radium Institute, and two years later her

book "La Radiologie et la guerre" was published. In

it she gave a most informative account of the

scientific and human experiences gained for

radiology (the use of radiation) during the war. At

the end of the war, her daughter Irène, a

physicist, was appointed as an assistant in her

mother's laboratory.

Shortly afterward, a momentous visit took

place in the Radium Institute. The visitor was Mrs.

William B. Meloney, editor of a leading magazine in

New York and representative of the countless

women who for years had found in Curie their

ideal and inspiration.

A year later Meloney returned to tell Curie

that a nationwide subscription in America had

produced the sum of one hundred thousand

dollars, which was needed to purchase a gram of

radium for her institute.

She was also asked to visit the United

States with her daughters and collect the

precious gift in person. Her trip was an absolute

triumph. In the White House, President Warren G.

Harding (1865-1923) presented her with the

golden key to the little metal box containing the

radium.

4
Fame

Marie and Pierre Curie at work in lab

Source: Wellcome Collection gallery (2018-03-31
Photographer: Unknown
License: CC BY 4.0

Poland, at the time, didn't permit higher education for women, so Curie's simple wish to continue hers was inadvertently an ambitious one. Finally, upon association with Flying University, an institution that was covertly admitting women students, Curie found a way to continue her education. Realising that Poland would soon be a dead end for further scientific training, Curie began planning her relocation to Paris. During this time, while her father assisted in arranging the finances, she continued educating herself through books and associations with learned people. It was only at the age of 24, in 1891, that Curie moved to

Paris – a decision that has now changed the face of science. How, you ask? In these radical ways:

She changed our understanding of atoms .It is a common misconception that Curie discovered radioactivity and even X-rays.What she really did, and of no less implication, was recognise the significance of these discoveries and dig deep in places that no one else in the scientific community thought important.

In 1895, a physicist named Wilhelm Roentgen discovered X-rays, and a year later, another prominent physicist, Henri Becquerel, discovered the existence of radioactivity. Becquerel found that Uranium emitted rays that were similar to X-rays but much weaker. He showed that these rays were not the result of a chemical reaction with the environment but that Uranium was producing them spontaneously. He also demonstrated that the emitted rays were electrically charging the air around the sample.

Curie thought these interesting enough for her thesis work.Using Becquerel's work as a template, she began examining Uranium samples. She used the storeroom of the Municipal School where Pierre Curie (they were now married) was a professor, as her lab. Together, they devised a way to measure more precisely the electrical changes that were being produced by Uranium.

With these measurements, Curie found that the

rays being emitted depended entirely on the

amount of Uranium – the total atoms in the

sample. She realised that the 'Becquerel rays' were

coming directly from the atoms.

This discovery was revelatory because until

then atoms were thought to be indivisible. But

Curie's theory of radioactive decay proved the

existence of subatomic particles. It showed that

unstable atoms could undergo changes (by

emitting energy and electrons) and could give rise

to completely different atoms as a result.

This radical theory was further stabilised in

1898 when, in the search for other radioactive

elements, the Curies discovered two new elements– Polonium and Radium, both highly radioactive.

Carbon dating – a method by which the age of the Earth, and all its elements and fossils, is measured – relies on these radioactive theories hypothesised by Curie.

Her discovery also paved the way for radiation therapy .To prove that these elements were indeed new, Curie had to isolate them and measure their atomic weights (the number that gives each element its identity).

It took her more than ten years to successfully isolate Radium, which she finally did in 1910. By then, she had already discovered that tumour cells, when exposed to radium, were destroyed faster than healthy cells.

During World War I, she invented a way to sterilise infected tissue using radium by means of hollow needles containing radioactive gas. She also set up radiology centers to assist military doctors at field hospitals, and developed mobile radiological units, then popularly known as 'petites Curies'.

These she installed after gaining an understanding of anatomy and even automotive mechanics, and after procuring X-ray machines and the necessary vehicles. Her radiological centers treated over a million soldiers during the war.

Although scientists now use different and safer methods for radiation therapy, what began with the discovery of X-rays picked up momentum only due to these efforts of Curie – however hazardous they may have been in retrospect.

She created a place for women in science

Due to her pioneering contributions and dedication to her work, Curie bagged several 'first woman' titles. In 1903, she became the first woman to win a Nobel Prize (Physics) and when she was awarded the Prize again in 1911, this time for Chemistry, she became the first woman to win it twice.After her husband died, she was offered his position in the University of Paris, making her the first woman to become a professor in that institution.

Curie never actively fought for these titles. Instead, she merely carried on with her scientific research – as seamlessly as the act of breathing – that spoke for itself. She did, however, use these titles and the respect they demanded to clear the path of her research.

Marie Curie is the example of what one can

achieve when there's genuine love for one's work.

Here's to the woman who walked undeterred, who

was so consumed by her love for science that her

bridal outfit, for all those years of scientific

discovery, took on the role of her laboratory

clothing.

Most challenging

To overcome the obstacles they faced,

Marie agreed to work as a tutor and children's

governess to support Bronya financially. This

allowed Bronya to go to France and study medicine

in Paris.

For the next few years of her life, Marie worked to earn money for herself and Bronya. In the evenings, if she had time, she studied chemistry, physics, and mathematics textbooks. She also attended lectures and laboratory practicals at an illegal free "university" where Poles learned about Polish culture and practical science, both of which had been suppressed by the Russian Tsarist authorities.

In November 1891, aged 24, Marie followed Bronya to Paris. There she studied chemistry, mathematics, and physics at the Sorbonne, Paris' most prestigious university. The course was, of course, taught in French, which Marie had to attain excellence in, very quickly.

At first she shared an apartment with Bronya and Bronya's husband, but the apartment was an hour away from the university. Marie decided to rent a room in the Latin Quarter, closer to the Sorbonne.

This was a time of hardship for the young scientist; winters in her unheated apartment chilled her to the bone.

Top Student Again

In summer 1893, aged 26, Marie finished as top student in her master's physics degree course.

She was then awarded industrial funding to

investigate how the composition of steel affected

its magnetic properties. The idea was to find ways

of making stronger magnets.

Her thirst for knowledge pushed her to continue

with her education: she completed a master's

degree in chemistry in 1894, aged 27.

Homesick

For a long time, Marie had been homesick.

She dearly wished to return to live in Poland.

After working in Paris on steel magnets for a year,

she vacationed in Poland, hoping to find work.

Unfortunately, there were no jobs for her.

A few years earlier, she had been unable to study for a degree in her homeland because she was a woman. Now, for the same reason, she found she could not get a position at a university.

Tragedy and Progress

The money from their Nobel Prizes made life easier for Marie and Pierre. For the first time, they could afford a laboratory assistant. Pierre took the Chair of Physics at the Sorbonne. The university also agreed to provide a new, well-equipped laboratory for the couple. In 1904, Marie and Pierre had a second daughter, Eve.

And then their happy life together came to an end. In 1906, Pierre died when he was hit by a horse-drawn carriage in the street.

Although distraught over her loss, Marie accepted the offer from the Sorbonne to replace Pierre as the Chair of Physics.

Again, she was breaking the mold: she had been the first woman to win a Nobel Prize, and now, she was the first female professor at the University of Paris.

Meeting Pierre Curie

One of Marie's professors arranged a research grant for her to study the magnetic properties and chemical composition of steel. In arranging for lab space, she was introduced to a young man named Pierre Curie. Pierre was a brilliant researcher himself and had invented several instruments for measuring magnetic fields and electricity. He arranged a tiny space for her at the Municipal School of Industrial Physics and Chemistry where he worked. The two were married in the summer of 1895.

Marie had been intrigued by the reports of Wilhelm Roentgen's discovery of X-rays and by Henri Becquerel's report of similar "rays"emitted from uranium ores. She decided to use Pierre's

instruments to measure the faint electrical

currents she detected in air that had been

bombarded with uranium rays. Her studies showed

that the effects of the rays were constant even

when the uranium ore was treated in different

ways. She confirmed Becquerel's observation that

greater amounts of uranium in an ore resulted in

more intense rays.

Then she stated a revolutionary hypothesis;

Marie believed that the emission of these rays

was an atomic property of uranium. If true, this

would mean that the accepted view of the atom as

the smallest possible fragment of matter was

false.

Radioactive

Marie next decided to test all of the many known chemical ores to see if any others would emit Becquerel rays. In 1898, she coined the term "radioactive" to describe materials that had this effect. Pierre was so interested in her research that he put his own work aside to help her. Together, they found that two ores, chalcolite and pitchblende, were much more radioactive than pure uranium. Marie suspected that these ores might contain as yet undiscovered radioactive elements.

Several tons of pitchblende were donated by

the Austrian government, but the space Marie was

using for a lab was too small. The Curies moved

their research to an old shed outside of the

school.Processing the ore was backbreaking

work.New protocols for separating the

pitchblende into its chemical components had to

be devised.Marie often worked late into the night

stirring huge cauldrons with an iron rod nearly as

tall as her.

Little by little, various components of the

ore were tested. The Curies found that two of the

chemical components, one containing mostly

bismuth and another containing mostly barium,

were strongly radioactive. In July 1898, the

Curies published their conclusion: the bismuth

compound contained a previously undiscovered

radioactive element that they named polonium,

after Marie's native country, Poland. By the end

of that year they had isolated a second

radioactive element they called radium, from

radius, the Latin word for rays. In 1902, they

announced success in extracting purified radium.

In June 1903, Marie was the first woman in

Europe to earn a doctorate in physics. In

November of that year, the Curies, together with

Henri Becquerel, were named winners of the Nobel

Prize in Physics for their contributions to the

understanding of atomic structure. The nominating

committee objected to including a woman as a

Nobel Laureate, but Pierre insisted that the

original research was Marie's. In 1911, after

Pierre's death, Marie was awarded a second Nobel

Prize in Chemistry for her discovery of the

elements polonium and radium.

A Ph.D. and a Nobel Prize in Physics!

In June 1903, Marie Curie was awarded her

Ph.D. by the Sorbonne. Her examiners were of the

view that she had made the greatest contribution

to science ever found in a Ph.D. thesis.

Six months later, the newly qualified researcher

was awarded the Nobel Prize in Physics!

She shared the prize with Pierre Curie and Henri Becquerel, the original discoverer of radioactivity.

The Nobel Committee were at first only going to give prizes to Pierre Curie and Henri Becquerel.

However, Pierre insisted that Marie must be honored. So, three people shared the prize for discoveries in the scientific field of radiation. Marie Curie was the first woman to be awarded a Nobel Prize.

Nobel Prize for Chemistry

In 1910, Marie isolated a pure sample of the metallic element radium for the first time. She had discovered the element 12 years earlier. In 1911, she was awarded the Nobel Prize for Chemistry for the "discovery of the elements radium and polonium, the isolation of radium and the study of the nature and compounds of this remarkable element."

Again, Marie Curie had broken the mold: she was the first person to win a Nobel Prize in both physics and chemistry. In fact, she is the only person ever to have done this.

5
Later life

The sudden death of Pierre Curie (April 19, 1906) was a bitter blow to Marie Curie, but it was also a decisive turning point in her career: from here on, she was to devote all her energy to completing alone the scientific work that they had undertaken. On May 13, 1906, she was appointed to the professorship that had been left vacant upon her husband's death; she was the first woman to teach in the Sorbonne.

In 1908, she became a professor and in 1910, her fundamental treatise on radioactivity was published. In 1911 she was awarded the Nobel Prize for Chemistry, for the isolation of pure radium.

In 1914, she saw the completion of the building of the laboratories of the Radium Institute (Institut du Radium) at the University of Paris.

In 1921, accompanied by her two daughters, Marie Curie made a triumphant journey to the United States, where President Warren G. Harding presented her with a gram of radium bought as the result of a collection among American women. She gave lectures, especially in Belgium, Brazil, Spain, and Czechoslovakia. She

was made a member of the International

Commission on Intellectual Co-operation by the

Council of the League of Nations. In addition, she

had the satisfaction of seeing the development of

the Curie Foundation in Paris and the inauguration

in 1932 in Warsaw of the Radium Institute, of

which her sister, Bronisława, became director.

One of Marie Curie's outstanding

achievements was to have understood the need to

accumulate intense radioactive sources, not only

to treat illness but also to maintain an abundant

supply for research in nuclear physics; the

resultant stockpile was an unrivaled instrument

until the appearance after 1930 of particle

accelerators.

The existence of a stock of 1.5 grams of radium at the Radium Institute in Paris, in which, over a period of several years, radium D and polonium had accumulated, made a decisive contribution to the success of the experiments undertaken in the years around 1930. Particularly of those performed by Irène Curie in conjunction with Frédéric Joliot, whom she had married in 1926 (see Joliot-Curie, Frédéric and Irène).

This work prepared the way for the discovery of the neutron by Sir James Chadwick and, above all, for the discovery in 1934 by Irène and Frédéric Joliot-Curie of artificial radioactivity.

6
Legacy

Marie Curie made many breakthroughs in her lifetime. Remembered as a leading figure in science and a role model for women, she has received numerous posthumous honors. Several educational and research institutions, and medical centers bear the Curie name, including the Curie Institute and the Pierre and Marie Curie University, later renamed UPMC.

In 1995, Marie and Pierre Curie's remains were interred in the Panthéon in Paris, the final resting place of France's greatest minds. Curie

became the first and one of only five women to be

laid to rest there. In late 2017, the Panthéon

hosted an exhibition to honor the 150th birthday

of the pioneering scientist.

In 1937, Ève Curie wrote the first of many

biographies devoted to her famous mother,

Madame Curie, which became a feature film a few

years later. The story of the Nobel laureate was

back on the big screen in 2017 with Marie Curie:

The Courage of Knowledge, featuring Polish

actress Karolina Gruszka. In 2018, it was

announced that Amazon Prime Video was

developing another biopic of Curie, with British

actress Rosamund Pike in the starring role.

Marie Curie died aged 66 on July 4, 1934, killed by aplastic anemia, a disease of the bone marrow. The radioactivity she was exposed to during her career probably caused the disease.

Scientists are now much more cautious in their handling of radioactive elements and X-rays than they were in the first few decades after their discovery. Marie Curie's own books and papers are so radioactive that they are now stored in lead boxes, which may only be opened by people wearing protective suits.

Marie Curie's Belongings Will Be Radioactive For Another 1,500 Years

Marie Curie, known as the 'mother of modern physics', died from aplastic anaemia, a rare condition linked to high levels of exposure to her famed discoveries, the radioactive elements polonium and radium.

Curie, the first and only woman to win a Nobel Prize in two different fields (physics and chemistry), furthered the research of French physicist Henri Becquerel, who in 1896 discovered that the element, uranium, emits rays.

Alongside her French physicist husband, Pierre Curie, the brilliant scientific pair discovered a new radioactive element in 1898. The duo named the element polonium, after Poland, Marie's native country.

Still, after more than 100 years, much of

Curie's personal effects including her clothes,

furniture, cookbooks, and laboratory notes are

still radioactive, author Bill Bryson writes in his

book, A Short History of Nearly Everything.

Regarded as national and scientific

treasures, Curie's laboratory notebooks are

stored in lead-lined boxes at France's Bibliotheque

National in Paris.

While the library grants access to visitors to view

Curie's manuscripts, all guests are expected to

sign a liability waiver and wear protective gear as

the items are contaminated with radium 226,

which has a half life of about 1,600 years,

according to Christian Science Monitor.

Her body is also radioactive and was

therefore placed in a coffin lined with nearly an

inch of lead.

The Curie's are buried in France's Panthéon,

a mausoleum in Paris which contains the remains

of distinguished French citizens - like

philosophers Rousseau and Voltaire.